© Aladdin Books Ltd 1987

Designed and produced by
Aladdin Books Ltd
70 Old Compton Street
London W1

Design   David West
Children's Book Design
Editorial Planning   Clark Robinson Limited
Editor   Bibby Whittaker
Researcher   Cecilia Weston-Baker
Illustrated by   Ron Hayward Associates

EDITORIAL PANEL
The author Keith Lye, has worked
as an editor and lecturer on
geography in Great Britain, Africa
and the United States.

The educational consultant, Peter
Thwaites, is Head of Geography at
Windlesham House School in
Sussex.

The editorial consultant, John Clark,
has contributed to many
information and reference books.

First published in the
United States in 1987 by
Gloucester Press
387 Park Avenue South
New York, NY 10016

ISBN 0-531-17065-9

Library of Congress Catalog
Card Number: 87-80457

Printed in Belgium

AFRICA

KEITH LYE

GLOUCESTER PRESS
London · New York · Toronto · Sydney

CONTENTS

How the maps work

This book has two kinds of maps. The physical map on page 5 shows what the land is like - indicating rivers (blue lines), mountain ranges (purple and dark brown), forests (dark green) and deserts (beige). The red line on the physical map divide the regions which are dealt with in the individual chapters. Therefore, the shape of a region on the physical map corresponds to the shape of the region's political map.

The political maps, such as that on page 10, show the boundaries and names of all the countries in a region. Black squares indicate the location of the capital cities. Arranged around the maps are the flags of each country, together with the type of government, name of the capital city, population and land area.

Animal Panel

Alongside the physical map is an illustrated panel of animals that can be found in Africa. Beneath each picture is the animal's common name and Latin name.

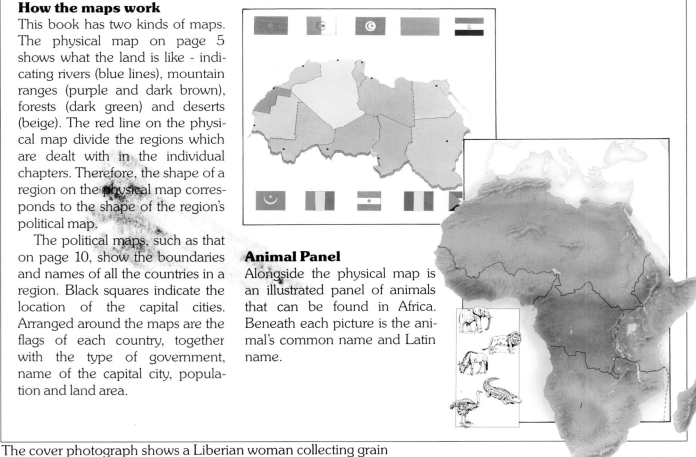

The cover photograph shows a Liberian woman collecting grain

INTRODUCTION

Africa is a fast-changing continent. Only 40 years ago, it was largely ruled by European countries. Today, most of its nations are independent, and many have adopted new names to reflect their changing character. The new Africa faces many problems. It is essentially a developing continent, and does not yet have the means to benefit from its vast natural resources.

One way of measuring a country's wealth is its per capita gross national product, or per capita GNP. This is the total value of the goods and services produced by a country in a year, divided by its population. South Africa, the continent's most developed country, had a per capita GNP of $2,500 in 1984. By comparison, Ethiopia is a poor, developing country with a per capita GNP of $110. However, some oil-rich countries have much higher per capita GNPs; for example, Libya's — $8,230. But this is not a developed country; it lacks the industry, communications and other services that are taken for granted in Western countries like the United States, whose per capita GNP in 1984 was $15,490.

Cheetahs — the fastest animals on land — hunt on the African savanna

AFRICA

Area: 30,330,000 sq km (11,710,000 sq miles).
Highest peak: Mount Kilimanjaro, Tanzania 5,895 m (19,341 ft).
Largest desert: Sahara, 9,065,000 sq km (3,500,000 sq miles).
Largest lake: Lake Victoria, 69,412 sq km (26,800 sq miles).
Longest river: Nile, 6,670 km (4,145 miles).

Africa is the second largest continent after Asia. Most of this land mass lies in the tropics and Africa is, therefore, the hottest continent. The rainfall varies greatly between the humid forest lands around the equator and the huge deserts to the north and south.

Africa has five main regions. *North Africa* contains fertile coastlands, but the Sahara Desert dominates this region. *West Africa* and *Central Africa* are hot and generally wet, with forests and savanna (tropical grassland). *East Africa* is a highland region with a pleasant climate, although it straddles the equator. *Southern Africa* also consists mainly of a high plateau. It includes deserts and grasslands called veld.

Land and climate

The height of the land greatly influences the climate of Africa. Because temperatures fall by 6-7°C for every 1,000 meters (about 14°F for every 3,000 feet) of altitude, highlands in the tropical regions have a cooler climate than nearby coastlands. Mount Kilimanjaro lies close to the equator but it is always capped by snow and ice. Below the snow line is a zone of tundra vegetation, then mountain grassland, forests and, at the bottom, savanna.

The eastern Sahara is one of the world's driest and sunniest places. It is crossed by the Nile, a river whose headstreams flow from the rainy highlands farther south. The irrigated Nile valley, one of Africa's most densely populated areas, was the site of the Ancient Egyptian civilization. The Nile is the world's longest river. Other African rivers, in order of length, are the Zaire (once called the Congo), the Niger and the Zambezi.

Snow-capped Mt. Kilimanjaro, near the equator

A felucca sails along the Nile near Aswan, Egypt

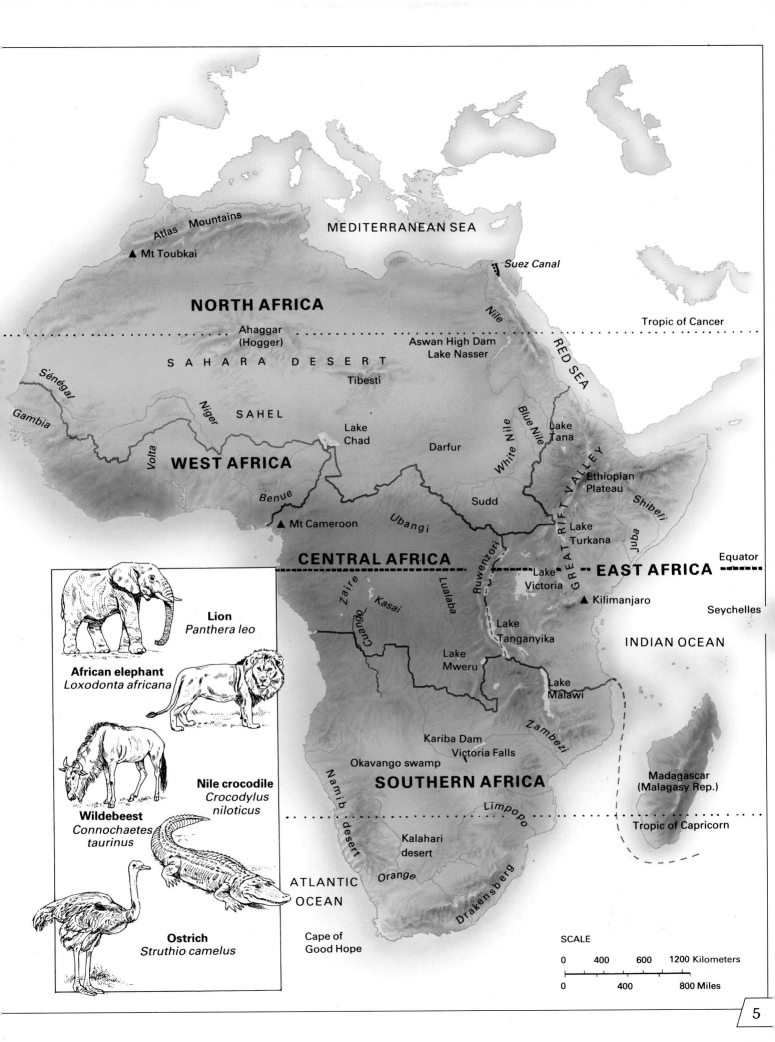

Atlas Mountains
▲ Mt Toubkai

MEDITERRANEAN SEA

Suez Canal

NORTH AFRICA

Tropic of Cancer

Ahaggar
(Hogger)

S A H A R A   D E S E R T

Aswan High Dam
Lake Nasser

Tibesti

Sénégal

Gambia

Niger

S A H E L

Volta

Lake
Chad

Darfur

WEST AFRICA

Benue

▲ Mt Cameroon

Ubangi

Sudd

White Nile

Blue Nile

Lake
Tana

RED SEA

Ethiopian
Plateau

Shibeli

CENTRAL AFRICA

Zaire

Kasai

Cuango

Lualaba

Ruwenzori

Lake
Victoria

GREAT RIFT VALLEY

Lake
Turkana

Juba

EAST AFRICA

Equator

▲ Kilimanjaro

Seychelles

Lion
Panthera leo

African elephant
Loxodonta africana

Lake
Tanganyika

Lake
Mweru

INDIAN OCEAN

Lake
Malawi

Nile crocodile
*Crocodylus
niloticus*

Wildebeest
*Connochaetes
taurinus*

Zambezi

Kariba Dam
Victoria Falls

Okavango swamp

Namib desert

SOUTHERN AFRICA

Madagascar
(Malagasy Rep.)

Limpopo

Tropic of Capricorn

Kalahari
desert

Ostrich
Struthio camelus

Orange

Drakensberg

ATLANTIC
OCEAN

Cape of
Good Hope

SCALE

0   400   600   1200 Kilometers

0   400   800 Miles

5

PLANTS AND ANIMALS

Deserts and grasslands each cover about two-fifths of Africa. Rain forests once grew along much of West Africa's coast, but they have been largely cleared by farmers. The biggest surviving rain forests are in the Zaire basin. Africa's grasslands have also been harmed by human activity. Some areas have been so overgrazed and overfarmed that they have become deserts. The destruction of natural habitats, combined with over-hunting, has also reduced the numbers of many of the animals, in some cases to near extinction. National Parks try to reverse this trend.

Plants

Between the equatorial rain forests and the deserts of Africa is a broad, hot zone with marked wet and dry seasons. It is covered by savanna, which is tropical grassland, with some trees such as acacias and baobabs. In the wetter regions, woodland savanna, with tall grasses, is common. Towards the deserts is a zone of dry savanna, with low grasses and few trees. In North Africa, this region is called the Sahel. It merges into a thorn bush zone and eventually into desert.

Much of the equatorial zone of West and Central Africa has high temperatures and plentiful rain throughout the year. For example, Libreville, Gabon, has an average annual temperature of 26°C (79°F) and an average yearly rainfall of 251 cm (99 inches). These conditions favor the growth of forests with tall trees and dark, shaded forest floors. Such forests contain hardwoods, including ebony and mahogany. Other valuable woods are okoumé and limba, used in the furniture industry.

Acacia trees growing on savanna grassland

A spectacular waterfall in an African tropical forest

Animals

Zoologists divide Africa into two zones. The Palaearctic zone includes the coasts along the Mediterranean, with their hot, dry summers and mild, moist winters. Zoologically, this zone is similar to Europe, with animals such as deer and wild boars. But most of Africa lies within the Ethiopian zone, so-called because all of Africa south of the Sahara was once called Ethiopia.

The Ethiopian zone contains many animal families which live only in Africa. It is rich in mammals. Excluding bats, it has 38 families of mammals, including many primates – monkeys, lemurs (especially in Madagascar) and great apes. Of the world's four species of great apes, two – chimpanzees and gorillas – live in Africa's forests. Another vegetation zone, the savanna, is rich in wildlife, including antelopes, buffaloes, elephants and zebras, together with predators such as cheetahs, leopards and lions. Crocodiles and hippopotamuses live in rivers and lakes, and birds abound wherever water is available. Some animals have even

The forests of Rwanda provide homes for gorillas

adapted to live in the driest deserts. The most familiar Saharan animal, the camel, is a comparative newcomer. It was introduced from Asia more than 2,000 years ago. The great range of wildlife in Africa attracts many tourists, who provide some nations with much-needed foreign income. Many countries have set up national parks where hunting is illegal and where tourists are able to observe many beautiful animals in their natural habitats.

Zebras and a herd of wildebeest in Tanzania

Lionesses and cubs feed on an antelope in Kenya

Population: 582,000,000.
Population density: 19 per sq km (50 per sq mile).
Population of largest cities:

Cairo, Egypt	14,000,000
Alexandria, Egypt	5,000,000
Algiers, Algeria	3,250,000
Lagos, Nigeria	3,000,000
Kinshasa, Zaire	2,500,000

The Sahara divides the people of Africa into two main groups. In North Africa, most people speak either Arabic or one of several Berber languages (see below). South of the Sahara, however, more than 1,000 languages and dialects are spoken.

Most black Africans, who make up four-fifths of Africa's population, live south of the Sahara. Some Asians and Europeans also live in Africa, mostly in the south and east. Their ancestors settled in Africa when the continent was colonized by European countries. The largest group of Europeans is in South Africa.

Ethnic groups

Berbers have lived in North Africa since prehistoric times. They include nomads, such as Tuaregs, who live in the Sahara, moving from one oasis (watering place) to another in search of pasture for their animals. Arabs invaded North Africa in the 7th century AD. They introduced the Arabic language ("Berber" was, in fact, a name given by the Arabs), and Islam, which is now the chief religion of North Africa. In the Middle Ages, Arab traders crossed the Sahara in camel caravans and converted people in West and Central Africa to Islam. Arabs also sailed to East Africa, where they made more converts.

The earliest known people in Southern Africa were hunters and gatherers. Their descendants are the Pygmies of the rain forests and the Bushmen of the Kalahari, a semi-desert in Southern Africa. Later, other black people migrated throughout Africa south of the Sahara. They founded some major medieval empires. European powers colonized most of Africa in the 19th century. They introduced Christianity, although local beliefs remained strong. In 1945, only Egypt, Ethiopia, Liberia and South Africa where not European colonies. But today almost all African countries are independent.

Tuaregs of Algeria traditionally wear black

Bushmen are skilled hunters with a bow and arrow

Evolution

Fossils of early creatures related to modern humans have been discovered in several parts of the world. But the greatest concentration of such fossils occurs in Africa. Some experts now believe that the evolutionary split between apes and humans probably occurred in East Africa, more than four million years ago. In recent times, East Africa has yielded many fossils of Australopithecines, who were among our earliest ancestors, as well as examples of other, later species: *Homo habilis*, *Homo erectus* and *Homo sapiens*.

Many fossils of *Australopithecus* have been found in East Africa.

Ways of life

Most African countries are poor. Almost two-thirds of the world's poorest countries (those with per capita GNPs of less than $400 in 1984) are in Africa. Farming employs more than three out of every five Africans. But most African farmers produce little more than they need to feed their families. When droughts occur, crops fail and livestock dies. Many people then starve. South Africa, where 56 per cent of the people live in cities and towns, is Africa's most developed country. But South African whites have a much higher standard of living than blacks.

Many Africans are moving to the cities to find jobs

A fertile farm in Liberia

NORTH AFRICA

Population: 152,868,000.
Area: 13,346,403 sq km (5,153,075 sq miles).
Population density: 11 per sq km (30 per sq mile).
Economy: The average per capita gross national product (1984) was $1,050; Libya's was the highest at $8,230, Chad's was the lowest at $88.

North Africa, which is by far the largest of the African regions, is largely desert and is thinly populated. All its ten countries are underdeveloped, although the northern five – Morocco, Algeria, Tunisia, Libya and Egypt – are called by the United Nations "middle income developing countries." By contrast, the southern five – Mauritania, Mali, Niger, Chad and Sudan – are among Africa's poorest. Most Northern Africans are Muslims (followers of the Islamic faith), and Arabic is an official language in all the countries except Mali and Niger, where French is used.

Morocco (inc. W. Sahara)
Monarchy
Cap: Rabat
Pop: 23,759,000
Area: 712,550 sq km
(275,117 sq mi)

Algeria
Democratic Republic
Cap: Algiers
Pop: 22,817,000
Area: 2,381,741 sq km
(919,595 sq mi)

Tunisia
Republic
Cap: Tunis
Pop: 7,424,000
Area: 163,610 sq km
(63,170 sq mi)

Libya
Socialist People's Republic
Cap: Tripoli
Pop: 3,876,000
Area: 1,759,540 sq km
(679,362 sq mi)

Egypt
Republic
Cap: Cairo
Pop: 50,525,000
Area: 1,001,449 sq km
(386,662 sq mi)

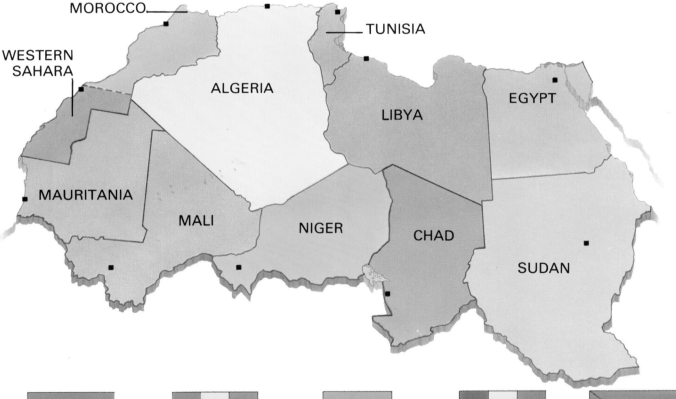

Mauritania
Islamic Republic
Cap: Nouakchott
Pop: 1,691,000
Area: 1,030,700 sq km
(397,956 sq mi)

Mali
Republic
Cap: Bamako
Pop: 7,898,000
Area: 1,240,000 sq km
(478,767 sq mi)

Niger
Republic
Cap: Niamey
Pop: 6,715,000
Area: 1,267,000 sq km
(489,191 sq mi)

Chad
Republic
Cap: N'Djamena
Pop: 5,231,000
Area: 1,284,000 sq km
(495,755 sq mi)

Sudan
Republic
Cap: Khartoum
Pop: 22,932,000
Area: 2,505,813 sq km
(967,500 sq mi)

Land and climate

The Sahara, which covers an area almost as large as the United States, occupies most of North Africa. The annual rainfall, outside of mountain regions, is less than 25 cm (10 inches). Temperatures are high. The world's record shade temperature – 58°C (136.4°F) – was recorded at Al Aziziyah, Libya. The northern Mediterranean coasts and northwestern Morocco, which faces the Atlantic, have dry, sunny summers, but enough rain falls in winter to make farming possible. The southern parts of Mauritania, Mali, Niger, Chad and Sudan also have enough rain for agriculture. For example, N'Djamena, near Lake Chad, has an average annual rainfall of 71 cm (28 inches). Sudan, which extends farther south than the other countries, is particularly arid in the north, which has less than 12 cm (5 inches) of rain per year. But the southern mountains get 152 cm (60 inches) or more.

Many mountains in North Africa, including the Ahaggar, Tibesti and Darfur massifs, are volcanic in origin. The Atlas Mountains, which run from Morocco through Algeria to Tunisia, are mountains that were forced upwards at the same time as the Alps when Africa pushed northwards against Europe.

Wine grapes are an important crop in Tunisia

Irrigation is essential in Libya's parched farmland

The Atlas Mountains form Morocco's southern border

11

Ways of life

Many North Africans once lived nomadic lives, moving around in search of food and pasture for their camels, goats, sheep and, in wetter areas, cattle. Others lived at fertile oases or in towns. The number of nomads has greatly declined in recent years. Droughts have caused enormous losses in livestock, while better job opportunities and standards of living in the growing cities have attracted people from rural areas.

Camels are still used as beasts of burden

Religion

Islam is the dominant religion in North Africa. In Sudan, 25 per cent of the population are southerners who follow either local religions or Christianity. The southerners oppose the enforcement of Islamic law in the south and they have fought a long civil war against government forces. Religious and ethnic differences have also contributed to unrest in Chad, where northern Muslims have been aided by Libya.

Islam is the chief religion in North Africa

Creeping desert

Sahara is the Arabic word for desert. Four-fifths of the Sahara is made up of areas of bare rock, called *hammada*, or by plains covered by gravel and pebbles, called *reg* or *serir*. Wind-blown sand covers the remaining fifth of the Sahara. Sandy deserts are called *erg*, another Arabic term.

Settlements around oases are under constant threat from shifting dunes, which are moved forward by winds blowing from only one direction. Dunes have buried many settlements, but this can be improved by planting grasses and trees, whose roots bind the sand together and stop it moving.

Wind shifts sand dunes

Sand encroaches on farmland

Farmland threatened

The Suez Canal

The Suez Canal links the Mediterranean Sea with the Red Sea

The completion of the Suez Canal (shown in red on the map) in 1869 gave international shipping a short cut between Europe and Asia. However, the Sinai peninsula and Suez region have been the scene of warfare between Egyptian and Israeli forces in 1948-9, 1956, 1967 and 1973. In the 1956 war, the Egyptians blocked the canal, but it was reopened in 1957. In 1967, however, it was again closed and did not reopen until 1975. In 1979, Egypt and Israel signed a peace treaty, despite opposition from most Muslim countries in North Africa and Southwestern Asia. As a result, Egypt's membership of the Arab League was suspended.

Arab unrest

Colonel Gaddafi is Libya's ruler

Libya's leader General Gaddafi has vigorously opposed Israel and supported the PLO (Palestine Liberation Organization) in its struggle to found an Arab state in what is now Israel. With its considerable income from oil sales, Libya has supported many nationalist movements around the world. In 1986, US aircraft bombed terrorist bases in Libya.

A continuing conflict in North Africa involves Western Sahara, which was once ruled by Spain. In 1976, Spain agreed that Morocco and Mauritania should take over. Mauritania withdrew in 1979 and Morocco took the entire territory. Saharan guerrillas have fought against Moroccans, claiming that they have set up their own independent republic.

Agriculture

The main crops in northern Africa include barley, rice, wheat, citrus fruits, dates, olives and cotton. Further south, cotton, millet and peanuts are important. South of the Sahara, the savanna of the Sahel had plenty of rain in the early 1960s. Many farmers increased the numbers of their cattle and other livestock. But from the late 1960s to 1980s, severe droughts occurred. The dry conditions, combined with overgrazing and the removal of trees for firewood, laid the soil bare. Winds moved the loose topsoil and turned large areas into desert. In places, the Sahara advanced southward by 50 km (31 miles) a year.

Date palms grow on irrigated land in Morocco

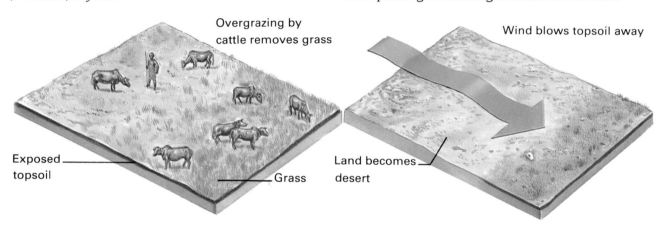

Overgrazing by cattle removes grass

Exposed topsoil

Grass

Wind blows topsoil away

Land becomes desert

Culture

The great civilization of Ancient Egypt rose to power about 5,000 years ago. Its economy was based on farming, made possible by irrigation. Until recently, the Nile regularly flooded its lower valley. Floods no longer occur because the river has been dammed at Aswan, where the water is now used to produce hydroelectricity. The floods once spread fertile silt over the land, but this silt now piles up on the floor of Lake Nasser, the huge artificial lake behind the dam. However, the benefits of a regulated flow of water are great.

The Ancient Egyptians had a complex religion based on the worship of many gods and goddesses. Christianity became important in Egypt from AD 300. But, following the Arab invasion in 639-642, most people became Muslims. Today, Christians make up fewer than 10 per cent of the population.

Egyptian pyramids date back 4,500 years

Economy

Egypt is Africa's second most industrialized nation, after South Africa. Egypt gets cheap electricity from the Aswan hydroelectric power stations, and it produces enough oil for its needs. Major products include cement, iron and steel, fertilizers and processed foods. In Algeria and Libya, income from oil and gas sales is being used to develop industries, especially petrochemicals and steel. Manufacturing is also steadily increasing in Morocco, while tourism is the mainstay of Tunisia's economy. In Mauritania, Mali, Niger, Chad and Sudan, farming employs 78 per cent of the workforce, compared with 41 per cent in the northern five countries of North Africa.

Steel is one of Egypt's major industries

Libya and Algeria are major oil and natural gas producers and exporters, and this makes them the most prosperous countries in North Africa. Tunisia and Egypt produce some oil and phosphates. Morocco is the world's third largest producer of phosphates, after the United States and the Soviet Union. One of Morocco's richest deposits is in Western Sahara. Mauritania is Africa's third leading producer of iron ore, and Niger's leading export is uranium. Mining is less important in Mali, Chad and Sudan. Sudan has some oil, but its development has been delayed because the oilfield lies in the southern area, which has been the scene of civil war.

Waste gas being burned off at oil wells in the Algerian desert

WEST AFRICA

Population: 164,828,000.
Area: 2,604,986 sq km (1,005,792 sq miles).
Population density: 63 per sq km (164 per sq mile).
Economy: The average per capita gross national product (1984) was $600; Nigeria's was highest at $770, Burkina Faso's was the lowest at $160.

West Africa's 13 nations form Africa's most densely populated region. Liberia was the only independent country until 1957, when it was joined by Ghana, followed by Guinea in 1958. Benin, Burkina Faso, Ivory Coast, Nigeria, Senegal and Togo became independent in 1960, Sierra Leone in 1961, Gambia in 1965, Guinea-Bissau in 1974, and Cape Verde in 1975. So many African languages and dialects are spoken in this region – Nigeria alone has 250 – that for the time being most countries have kept European colonial languages as their official ones.

Senegal
Republic
Cap: Dakar
Pop: 6,980,000
Area: 196,192 sq km
(75,750 sq mi)

Gambia
Republic
Cap: Banjul
Pop: 774,000
Area: 11,295 sq km
(4,361 sq mi)

Guinea-Bissau
Republic
Cap: Bissau
Pop: 875,000
Area: 36,152 sq km
(13,948 sq mi)

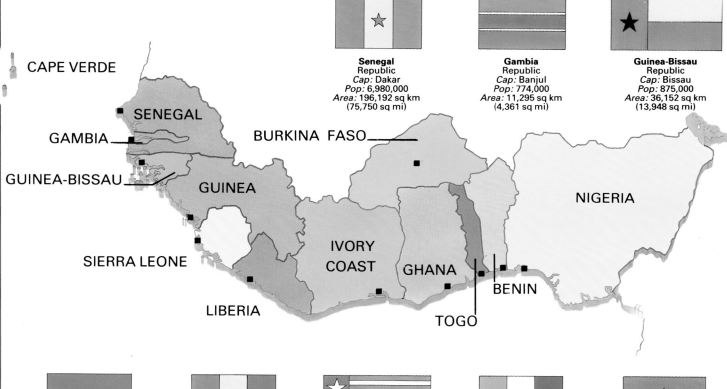

CAPE VERDE

SENEGAL

GAMBIA

BURKINA FASO

GUINEA-BISSAU

GUINEA

NIGERIA

IVORY COAST

GHANA

BENIN

SIERRA LEONE

TOGO

LIBERIA

Sierra Leone
Republic
Cap: Freetown
Pop: 3,987,000
Area: 71,740 sq km
(27,699 sq mi)

Guinea
Republic
Cap: Conakry
Pop: 5,734,000
Area: 245,857 sq km
(94,926 sq mi)

Liberia
Republic
Cap: Monrovia
Pop: 2,307,000
Area: 111,369 sq km
(43,000 sq mi)

Ivory Coast
Republic
Cap: Abidjan
Pop: 10,500,000
Area: 322,463 sq km
(124,504 sq mi)

Burkina Faso
Republic
Cap: Ouagadougou
Pop: 7,094,000
Area: 274,200 sq km
(105,869 sq mi)

Ghana
Republic
Cap: Accra
Pop: 13,552,000
Area: 238,537 sq km
(92,100 sq mi)

Togo
Republic
Cap: Lomé
Pop: 3,118,000
Area: 56,785 sq km
(21,925 sq mi)

Benin
People's Republic
Cap: Porto Novo
Pop: 4,141,000
Area: 112,622 sq km
(43,484 sq mi)

Nigeria
Federal Republic
Cap: Lagos
Pop: 105,448,000
Area: 923,768 sq km
(356,669 sq mi)

Cape Verde
Republic
Cap: Praia
Pop: 318,000
Area: 4,033 sq km
(1,557 sq mi)

Young cocoa plants for a plantation in Senegal

A stockaded village in the Sahel, Burkina Faso

The coasts of West Africa are varied. Marshes border the Niger River delta, with lagoons in western Nigeria and Ivory Coast. Abidjan, the capital of Ivory Coast, stands on a lagoon. It is linked to the sea by a canal cut through a sandbank. In the west, the jagged coast is lined by islands, with some deep inlets cutting into the mainland. These inlets are former river valleys flooded by the sea. Inland there is a plateau. The uplands of Guinea and Sierra Leone contain the source of the Niger River. Another upland region, the Jos plateau, is in northern Nigeria.

West Africa lies in the tropics and is hot throughout the year. Rainfall is heaviest along the coast. For example, Lagos in Nigeria has an average annual rainfall of 184 cm (72 inches) and Abidjan 196 cm (77 inches). Dense forest once covered much of the coastal plain, although the forests have been largely replaced by farms and plantations, whose major products are cocoa, coffee, palm oil and rubber. Beyond the humid coastal plains the interior has a marked dry season in winter. This region is covered by savanna grasslands, including part of the Sahel in the north.

Abidjan is the thriving capital of Ivory Coast

Music and art

Music and dancing are major art forms in Africa south of the Sahara. African music was taken to the Americas by slaves, and its exciting rhythms have contributed to the development of modern Western music. West Africa is also known for its literature and sculpture. Some sculpture, such as wooden masks, was made for religious ceremonies. But superb bronzes and gold objects have also been produced, particularly in Nigeria, where the court art of two kingdoms – Ife, in the 12th-14th centuries, and later, Benin – have become world famous. African art, like its music, has influenced many artists in other countries.

Dancers in Ghana wear brightly colored robes

Recent history

West Africa has had a troubled history since the 1950s. Independence has brought many problems while governments have strived, often without success, to raise living standards. Most West African countries have experienced several military coups, or attempted coups, and most countries have resorted to setting up strong central governments, run by a single political party. Even Ivory Coast, which is among the most successful economically of the West African countries and which has survived without military governments, has resorted to one-party rule. By the late 1980s, only Gambia, Liberia and Senegal had more than one political party.

An overcrowded suburb on the edge of Freetown, capital of Sierra Leone

Nigeria is a major producer of oil and natural gas

Rubber is grown on plantations in Liberia

West Africa has important natural resources. Nigeria is Africa's chief oil producer. Guinea produces bauxite (aluminum ore); Liberia, iron ore; Sierra Leone, diamonds; Togo and Senegal, phosphates; and Ghana, gold and diamonds. Most manufacturing is small scale, with factories processing farm products or making things such as clothes and footwear. Farming employs 69 per cent of the work-force. Food crops include cassava, rice, sweet potatoes and yams in wet areas, and corn and millet in savanna regions. Huge numbers of cattle, goats and sheep graze on the savanna. The chief export crops are cocoa, coffee, cotton, palm products, peanuts and rubber. Several countries depend on one or two of these crops or resources. When world prices fall or crops fail, the countries have severe economic problems.

Iron ore being loaded onto railroad cars

CENTRAL AFRICA

Population: 47,423,000.
Area: 4,082,517 sq km (1,576,269 sq miles).
Population density: 11 per sq km (30 per sq mile).
Economy: The average per capita gross national product (1984) was $390; Gabon's was the highest at $3,690, Zaire's was the lowest at $200.

Central Africa contains seven nations, including Zaire which is one third the size of the United States, and the tiny nation of São Tomé and Príncipe. Forest covers large areas and the region is thinly populated. Central Africa has many ethnic groups, each with its own language or dialect. The official languages are European – French and English in Cameroon; French in the Central African Republic, Congo, Gabon and Zaire; Spanish in Equatorial Guinea; and Portuguese in São Tomé and Príncipe.

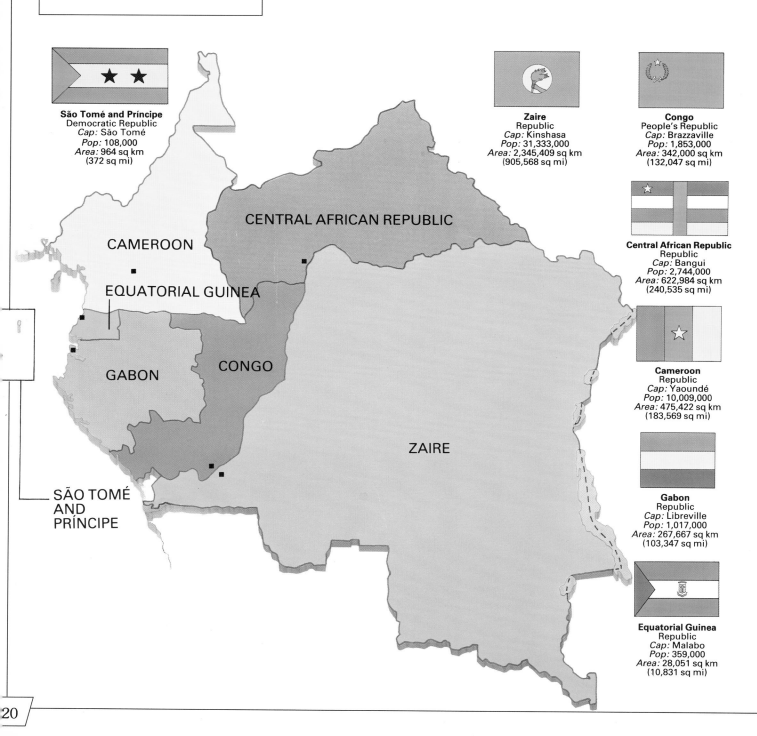

São Tomé and Príncipe
Democratic Republic
Cap: São Tomé
Pop: 108,000
Area: 964 sq km
(372 sq mi)

Zaire
Republic
Cap: Kinshasa
Pop: 31,333,000
Area: 2,345,409 sq km
(905,568 sq mi)

Congo
People's Republic
Cap: Brazzaville
Pop: 1,853,000
Area: 342,000 sq km
(132,047 sq mi)

Central African Republic
Republic
Cap: Bangui
Pop: 2,744,000
Area: 622,984 sq km
(240,535 sq mi)

Cameroon
Republic
Cap: Yaoundé
Pop: 10,009,000
Area: 475,422 sq km
(183,569 sq mi)

Gabon
Republic
Cap: Libreville
Pop: 1,017,000
Area: 267,667 sq km
(103,347 sq mi)

Equatorial Guinea
Republic
Cap: Malabo
Pop: 359,000
Area: 28,051 sq km
(10,831 sq mi)

CENTRAL AFRICAN REPUBLIC

CAMEROON

EQUATORIAL GUINEA

GABON

CONGO

ZAIRE

SÃO TOMÉ AND PRÍNCIPE

Land and climate

Central Africa has a hot, wet equatorial climate. For example, Kisangani, a port on the Zaire River, has an average annual temperature of 25°C (77°F) and an average yearly rainfall of 170 cm (67 inches). Rain forests cover regions near the equator, with open woodland and savanna to the north and south.

Central Africa is drained by huge rivers, notably the Zaire, which was once named the Congo. Its major tributaries include the Ubangi in the north, the Lualaba in the southeast, and the Kasai in the southwest. Waterfalls and rapids interrupt the upper courses of the rivers, but much of the middle and lower courses are navigable. Below Kinshasa, the Zaire River tumbles off the African plateau over a series of waterfalls and rapids, before reaching Matadi, Zaire's main port.

The number of rivers, tributaries and swamps, make much of the area impassable to trucks and trains. Instead the rivers are used as major transportation routes.

The Zaire River is a major transportation route

Most of Central Africa is part of a huge plateau which forms the interior of equatorial and southern Africa. Volcanic peaks rise in Cameroon. The highest volcano, Mount Cameroon, is one of Africa's wettest places. The annual rainfall sometimes exceeds 1,000 cm (nearly 410 inches). The islands of São Tomé and Príncipe, and Bioko in Equatorial Guinea, are also volcanic. High ranges border the East African region to the east of Zaire. Lying on the Eastern border of Zaire are, from south to north, lakes Tanganyika, Kivu, Edward and Mobutu Sese Seko. Towering above the lakes are blocks of land which have been pushed up by movements in the Earth's crust to form ranges such as the Ruwenzori in the northeast.

Clouds over the forests on the slopes of Mount Cameroon

Recent history

Central Africa faces problems of instability caused by the many ethnic and language groups. Some people want to set up their own countries. When Zaire became independent in 1960, civil war broke out. The fighting was severe in the mineral-rich province of Shaba in the south. Zaire has had a strong central government and only one political party since the 1960s. The other Central African countries also permit only one party. Two of them, Central African Republic and Equatorial Guinea, suffered under brutal dictators, both of whom were overthrown in 1979.

Many people in Central Africa are Christians, although many others follow local religions or forms of Christianity influenced by local beliefs. One famous Christian missionary, Dr Albert Schweitzer, built a hospital at Lambaréné, Gabon. He was awarded the Nobel Peace Prize in 1952.

Emperor Bokassa of the Central African Republic

Albert Schweitzer's hospital at Lambaréné, Gabon

Peoples

Pygmies are dwarf-like, dark-skinned people who live in remote forest areas in Cameroon, Congo, Gabon and Zaire, with a few others in Burundi and Rwanda in East Africa. They move around the forests, hunting animals and collecting plant foods. Pygmies once lived in a much larger area, but from about 100 BC, they were displaced by more advanced people who used iron tools and weapons. These people, who originated in the Cameroon area, spoke languages belonging to the Bantu family. They gradually spread throughout Central, Eastern and Southern Africa. Several hundred Bantu languages and dialects are spoken in Central Africa – Cameroon and Zaire have about 200 each.

Pygmies in the Central African Republic

Economy

Farming, fishing and forestry employ 71 per cent of the working people of Central Africa. Many farmers use a type of cultivation called shifting agriculture. This involves clearing a patch of forest or grassland, growing crops for a few years, and then moving on when the soil begins to lose its fertility. Using simple hand tools, many farmers produce little more than they need to feed their families. Major food crops include cassava, corn , millet, plantains (a kind of green banana), sweet potatoes and yams. Crops grown for export are produced mostly on large plantations. They include cocoa, cotton and palm products. Forestry is also important in areas where logs can be floated down the rivers.

Copper ore is a major mineral product of Zaire

Zaire is famous for its elaborate textile patterns

Central Africa is a poor region, but it does have valuable natural resources. Although mining is unimportant in Equatorial Guinea, Zaire is rich in minerals, including copper, diamonds and cobalt. Oil makes up more than four-fifths of the exports of Congo and Gabon, and oil is important in the economy of Cameroon. Gabon also produces manganese and uranium, and it has large, untapped iron ore reserves. The Central African Republic produces diamonds, and cocoa makes up 90 per cent of the exports of São Tomé and Príncipe. Most countries export their ores, because they lack industries to process them and to make metal and other products. The cities have small factories to process foods and sawmills for the timber. There are also many factories that make everyday items, such as cigarettes, clothing and soap.

EAST AFRICA

Population: 133,658,000.
Area: 4,291,035 sq km (1,656,778 sq miles).
Population density: 31 per sq km (81 per sq mile).
Economy: The average per capita gross national product (1984) was $210; Seychelles had the highest at $2,300, and Ethiopia the lowest at $110.

East Africa consists of 12 nations. Apart from Ethiopia, which was invaded by Italy and held for five years from 1936, the region remained colonized and under European rule until recently. Today, only the French Indian Ocean islands of Mayotte and Réunion are not independent. Except for Ethiopia and Somalia, all of the East African countries use English or French for official purposes, although some have also introduced a second, local official language. For example, Kenya and Tanzania use both English and Swahili as official languages.

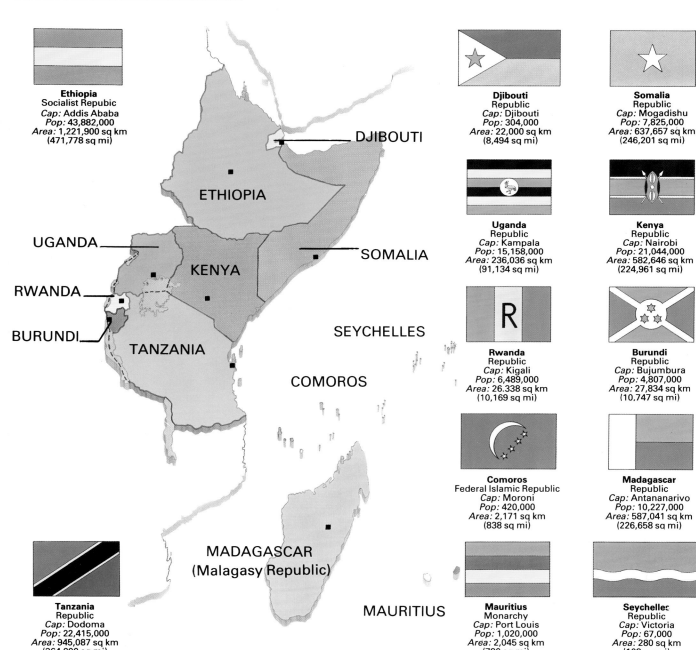

Ethiopia
Socialist Repubic
Cap: Addis Ababa
Pop: 43,882,000
Area: 1,221,900 sq km
(471,778 sq mi)

Djibouti
Republic
Cap: Djibouti
Pop: 304,000
Area: 22,000 sq km
(8,494 sq mi)

Somalia
Republic
Cap: Mogadishu
Pop: 7,825,000
Area: 637,657 sq km
(246,201 sq mi)

Uganda
Republic
Cap: Kampala
Pop: 15,158,000
Area: 236,036 sq km
(91,134 sq mi)

Kenya
Republic
Cap: Nairobi
Pop: 21,044,000
Area: 582,646 sq km
(224,961 sq mi)

Rwanda
Republic
Cap: Kigali
Pop: 6,489,000
Area: 26.338 sq km
(10,169 sq mi)

Burundi
Republic
Cap: Bujumbura
Pop: 4,807,000
Area: 27,834 sq km
(10,747 sq mi)

Comoros
Federal Islamic Republic
Cap: Moroni
Pop: 420,000
Area: 2,171 sq km
(838 sq mi)

Madagascar
Republic
Cap: Antananarivo
Pop: 10,227,000
Area: 587,041 sq km
(226,658 sq mi)

Tanzania
Republic
Cap: Dodoma
Pop: 22,415,000
Area: 945,087 sq km
(364,900 sq mi)

Mauritius
Monarchy
Cap: Port Louis
Pop: 1,020,000
Area: 2,045 sq km
(790 sq mi)

Seychelles
Republic
Cap: Victoria
Pop: 67,000
Area: 280 sq km
(108 sq mi)

Land and Climate

Running through the East African highlands is a deep valley formed when long blocks of land sank down between huge faults (cracks) in the Earth's crust. Called the Rift Valley, it contains many lakes, such as Lake Nakuru and Lake Naivasha in Kenya, but the largest lake in Africa, Lake Victoria, is not in the valley. The Rift Valley extends north through Ethiopia and includes the Red Sea and the Dead Sea. Along the valley are mountain ranges and some volcanic peaks, including Mount Kenya and Kilimanjaro, Africa's highest point.

East Africa's coastlands are hot throughout the year. Inland is a high, much cooler plateau, with mountains in places. For example, the Kenyan port of Mombasa has an average annual temperature of 26°C (79°F), as compared with 19°C (66°F) in Nairobi, Kenya's capital on the interior plateau. Much of East Africa is arid. The highlands of Ethiopia (the source of the Blue Nile River), Uganda (the source of the White Nile), Burundi and Rwanda generally have abundant rain. But the lowlands of Ethiopia, Somalia and northern Kenya are

A Kenyan village; the Rift Valley in the background

desert or semi-desert. Only 15 per cent of Kenya and 25 per cent of Tanzania can rely on up to 76 cm (30 inches) of rain each year. Madagascar has rain forest in the east, savanna in the center, and desert in the southwest.
coasts of East Africa are varied.

There are reefs with their colorful display of tropical fish and corals. Also on the coast lagoons have been formed by the silt washed down by the rivers. Waves and currents push against the flow of the river. The silt makes sandy spits.

The Blue Nile River flows northward through Ethiopia

How a lagoon is formed

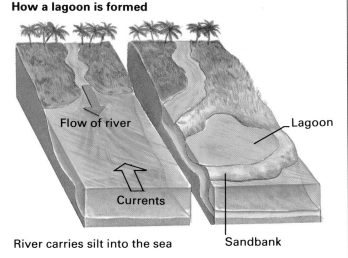

Flow of river

Currents

River carries silt into the sea

Lagoon

Sandbank

Recent history

East Africa's unreliable rainfall often causes crop failures. Long droughts, such as the ones that affected Ethiopia and Sudan in the 1970s and 1980s, prevent farmers from growing food and cause starvation and deaths among livestock and people. International relief organizations, governments of richer countries and individual people have given food and money to rescue thousands of starving Africans. But the threat of famine is ever present and has now reached Somalia.

Ethnic language differences have also caused conflict in East Africa. For example, Uganda has about 40 language groups and some of the smaller groups fear domination by the largest one, the Baganda. Conflict between the Hutu and Tutsi in Burundi and Rwanda has also led to much bloodshed. Such differences threaten national unity. For this reason, nine East African countries have adopted one-party governments.

People near to starvation after a drought

Uganda still has buildings from its colonial past

Language and religion

The people of East Africa have various languages and religions. Two main language families are used in the north: Semitic (which includes Amaharic, Ethiopia's official language) and Cushitic, including Somali. Most languages south of Somalia belong to the Bantu family, but Malagasy – spoken in Madagascar – is of Indonesian origin. Ethiopia adopted Christianity in the 4th century AD and its Coptic Church survived competition with Islam. The Somalis are Muslims, but to the south most people follow local religions or Christianity.

A Coptic priest in Ethiopia carries a ceremonial umbrella

Economy

East Africa has a lower per capita GNP than any other African region. Farming employs 74 per cent of the work force and many farmers are extremely poor. The poverty of most people is shown in the low average life expectancy. For example, Ethiopians live, on average, 44 years, whereas Kenyans live to an average age of 55. By comparison, the average life expectancy in Western countries is more than 70 years.

One major food crop in East Africa is corn. It is dried, ground into flour, cooked and often eaten with beans. Other food crops include various grains, cassava, rice and sweet potatoes.

Coffee, which originated in Ethiopia and still grows wild there, is a major export, together with bananas, copra, cotton and tea. The Comoros produce vanilla; Mauritius, sugar; and the Seychelles, copra and cinnamon. Livestock are grazed in the savanna regions, although tsetse flies, which carry disease, make large areas unsuitable for cattle. Mining is generally unimportant, although Rwanda produces tin and Tanzania has diamonds, while Uganda has reserves of copper and phosphates. Manufacturing is mostly confined to processing farm products and making ordinary household goods, including clothes.

Workers on a tea plantation

Cattle are a chief source of milk, meat and hides in Madagascar

SOUTHERN AFRICA

Population: 83,247,000.
Area: 6,003,387 sq km (2,317,922 sq miles).
Population density: 14 per sq km (36 per sq mile).
Economy: The average per capita gross national product (1984) was $1,170. South Africa had the highest at $2,500 and Mozambique had the lowest at $150.

Southern Africa consists of nine independent countries and Namibia, which is ruled by South Africa – Africa's most developed and prosperous nation. South Africa, which was formed in 1910, and Namibia have two official languages – Afrikaans, which developed from the Dutch spoken by the early settlers in the 17th century, and English. Other official languages reflecting colonial influence are Portuguese in Angola and Mozambique, English in Botswana, Swaziland, Zambia and Zimbabwe, English and Sesotho in Lesotho, and English and Chichewa in Malawi.

Angola
People's Republic
Cap: Luanda
Pop: 8,164,000
Area: 1,246,700 sq km
(481,354 sq mi)

Zambia
Republic
Cap: Lusaka
Pop: 7,054,000
Area: 752,614 sq km
(290,586 sq mi)

Malawi
Republic
Cap: Lilongwe
Pop: 7,292,000
Area: 118,484 sq km
(45,747 sq mi)

Botswana
Republic
Cap: Gaborone
Pop: 1,104,000
Area: 600,372 sq km
(231,805 sq mi)

Mozambique
People's Republic
Cap: Maputo
Pop: 14,022,000
Area: 801,590 sq km
(309,496 sq mi)

Swaziland
Monarchy
Cap: Mbabane
Pop: 692,000
Area: 17,363 sq km
(6,704 sq mi)

Namibia
S. African-ruled
Cap: Windhoek
Pop: 1,142,000
Area: 824,292 sq km
(318,261 sq mi)

Lesotho
Monarchy
Cap: Maseru
Pop: 1,552,000
Area: 30,355 sq km
(11,720 sq mi)

South Africa
Republic
Cap: Cape Town (Legislative)
Pop: 33,241,000
Area: 1,221,037 sq km
(471,445 sq mi)

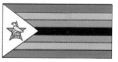

Zimbabwe
Republic
Cap: Harare
Pop: 8,984,000
Area: 390,580 sq km
(150,804 sq mi)

Land and climate

The northern part of the region is in the tropics. The coasts are hot throughout the year but the inland plateau is cooler. The southern part of the area is outside the tropics, but still has a generally warm climate. Many areas are dry. Southern Africa includes the Namib Desert and the Kalahari, a semi-desert located mostly in Botswana. The area around Cape Town in South Africa has a climate like that of the Mediterranean, with hot, dry summers and mild, moist winters.

The plateau which covers most of Central and Southern Africa reaches its highest point in the Drakensberg Mountains. This range is made up of the southeastern rim of the plateau. The main rivers of Southern Africa are the Zambezi, which plunges over the huge Victoria Falls, and the westward-flowing Orange River.

The Victoria Falls, Zimbabwe – named after the British Queen

Shrubs struggle to survive in the Namib desert

How gullies are formed

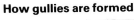
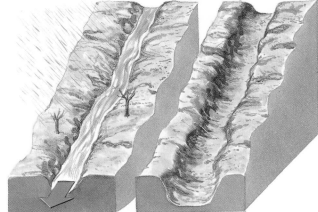

Floodwater after rain   Deep wadi in the dry season

The Namib desert on the coast of Namibia is one of the world's most barren regions. It contains huge areas of sand, where few living things can survive.

Much of the Kalahari has 25-50 cm (10-20 inches) of rain each year. Large areas are covered by grass and thorny shrubs. There is even the huge Okavango swamp in northern Botswana.

Many valleys in deserts were formed by rivers at a time when the climate was much much wetter than it is today. Running water still shapes desert scenery. This occurs during storms, when flood water pours down hollows carving out deep wadis (gullies). After a heavy downpour, no more rain may fall for a year or more.

The mild, warm climate of much of Southern Africa attracted many European settlers, including missionaries who converted many people to Christianity. Other newcomers were traders and prospectors, but most were farmers. Many whites settled in Zimbabwe, formerly the British colony of Rhodesia. The colony's government was run by the white settlers, although they made up only about 5 per cent of the population. In the early 1960s, the whites wanted independence, but Britain refused unless the black Africans were allowed to share the government. In 1965, the whites declared the country independent, an act which Britain condemned. A guerrilla war began in the early 1970s. In 1980 the country became independent, with black Africans forming the majority of the government. The prime minister was the former guerrilla leader, Robert Mugabe.

Cotton is a major export crop in Zimbabwe

Many blacks work in the South African gold mines.

The black township of Soweto in Johannesburg, S.A.

In South Africa, whites make up 18 per cent of the population, black Africans 70 per cent, Coloreds (of mixed origin) 9 per cent, and Asians 3 per cent. The whites control the government, although Coloreds and Asians were given some say from 1984. The blacks have few rights under South Africa's policy of separate development (apartheid). The government has reserved 13 per cent of the country as black Homelands. These areas are mostly poor, with infertile land. Most blacks oppose these racial policies and the United Nations has asked all countries to restrict trade with South Africa. The International Court of Justice has also ruled that South Africa's rule over Namibia is illegal.

Recent history

Angola and Mozambique once belonged to Portugal. In 1964, when the territories of Malawi and Zambia became independent, black Africans in Mozambique started a guerrilla war. Gradually, they took control of much of the country. In 1974 Portugal's government was overthrown, and Mozambique became independent in 1975. Many white settlers left and went to Portugal or South Africa. The new black government of Mozambique followed Socialist policies, and was the only political party permitted.

However, a black resistance movement called the MNR, supported by South Africa, is now fighting a guerrilla war against the government. Warfare and droughts caused severe food shortages in 1987.

Troops in Maputo, Mozambique

A Portuguese soldier in Angola

Angola, like Mozambique, became independent in 1975. In the struggle for independence, the black Africans (who speak Bantu languages) were divided into several opposing groups. The central government was finally formed by groups in central Angola, including the Mbundu and people of mixed descent. Another organization, UNITA, was supported by the largest group in the south, the Ovimbundu. After independence, UNITA forces launched a civil war against government troops, who included soldiers from Cuba.

Another problem occurred in southern Angola, where Namibians opposed to South African rule set up military bases. In 1983 South African troops invaded southern Angola and attacked the Namibians. South Africa also supported UNITA in its war against Angola's socialist government.

Culture

The culture of Southern Africa is very varied. The white Government in South Africa supports performing acts such as ballet, theatre and opera. Books are written mainly in Afrikaans or English, and many writers, such as Doris Lessing and J M Coetzee, have recently concentrated on the conflicts arising from apartheid. In recent times black writers have also begun to work within this tradition. Black culture is extremely rich. Many tribes, such as the Zulu, produce highly ornate headdresses, and their dances are based on religious situations or war dances. Primitive cave paintings can also be found in Southern Africa. These are attributable to the earliest inhabitants of the region, descendants of whom include the Bushmen (San).

Zulu dancers in traditional dress, South Africa

Agriculture

Farm workers tend a crop of corn in Zimbabwe

Farming employs about half of Southern Africa's work force, ranging from 86 per cent in Lesotho to 30 per cent in South rugged uplands are used for grazing huge numbers of cattle, sheep and goats. Botswana's chief farm product is beef, Lesotho exports wool and mohair, and Namibia also has many livestock products. Angola grows coffee and sisal; Malawi, tobacco and tea; Zambia, tobacco; Zimbabwe, cotton, tobacco and sugar; and Mozambique, cashew nuts. South African farms yield a wide range of products, including corn, meat, peanuts, sugar cane and a variety of vegetables, fruits and other export crops.

Economy

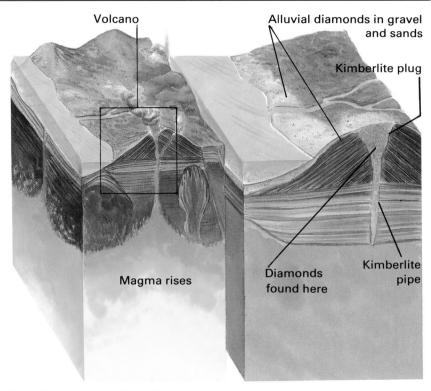

Volcano

Alluvial diamonds in gravel and sands

Kimberlite plug

Magma rises

Diamonds found here

Kimberlite pipe

How diamonds are formed

South Africa and Namibia are among the world's top producers of gem-quality diamonds. Other African diamond producers include Botswana, Angola and Lesotho. Diamond, which is chemically a pure form of carbon, is the hardest natural substance. Diamonds are formed under great pressure deep inside the Earth. They are found in rock formations called kimberlite pipes. These rocks are of volcanic origin and have been forced up to the surface through fissures (openings) in the overlying rocks. Some kimberlite pipes are mined, but some diamonds are also found in the sand and gravel on river beds. These alluvial diamonds have been worn away from the kimberlite pipes and washed into the streams by rain.

Cape Town, South Africa, is a busy port

Zambia has the world's biggest copper refinery

Southern Africa has many other natural resources besides diamonds. Angola is the only oil producer, although Botswana, Mozambique and Swaziland have some coal. Botswana also produces copper and nickel. Swaziland and Zimbabwe mine asbestos, while Zimbabwe also exports chrome, copper, gold, nickel and tin. Copper accounts for more than 90 per cent of Zambia's exports. Namibia exports lead, tin, uranium and zinc. South Africa is the world's leading producer of gold and chromite and is also Africa's top producer of asbestos, coal, iron ore, manganese, nickel, silver, uranium and zinc. Most manufacturing is small scale, except in Zimbabwe and, especially, South Africa. Manufacturing in South Africa includes cars, fertilizers, steel and other metals, machinery and textiles. Industrial areas include the Witwatersrand (the region around Johannesburg), and South Africa's main ports. With its highly efficient farms, its many natural resources and its industries, South Africa is the continent's leading economic power.

ORGANIZATIONS

The Arabic-speaking countries of North Africa belong to the Arab League. Egypt's membership was suspended in 1979 when it signed a peace treaty with Israel, against the wishes of the other league members. The leading African oil producers belong to OPEC (Organization of Petroleum Exporting Countries). OPEC has sought control over the production and prices of oil so that its members obtain the greatest benefit from oil sales. It was successful at first, but the fall in demand for oil in the 1980s – the result of a world economic recession – made it less effective.

Africa's political problems are discussed by the Organization of African Unity, which is made up of representatives of the governments of 49 African countries. (Morocco resigned in 1984 because of criticism of its rule in Western Sahara). The aims of the OAU are to promote unity, to raise living standards, to defend each country's territory and to oppose colonialism and racialism.

The OAU headquarters – Addis Ababa, Ethiopia

ARAB LEAGUE
Algeria
Bahrain
Djibouti
Iraq
Jordan
Kuwait
Lebanon
Libya
Mauritania
Morocco
Oman & PLO
Qatar
Saudi Arabia

Somalia
Sudan
Syria
Tunisia
UAE
North Yemen
South Yemen
OAC
Algeria
Angola
Benin
Botswana
Burkina Faso
Burundi

Cameroon
Cape Verde
Central African Rep.
Chad
Camoros
Congo
Djibouti
Egypt
Equatorial Guinea
Ethiopia
Gabon
Gambia
Ghana
Guinea

Guinea-Bissau
Ivory Coast
Kenya
Lesotho
Liberia
Libya
Madagascar
Malawi
Mali
Mauritania
Mauritius
Mozambique
Niger
Nigeria

Rwanda
São Tomé & Principe
Senegal
Seychelles
Sierra Leone
Somalia
Sudan
Swaziland
Tanzania
Togo
Tunisia
Uganda
Zaire
Zambia
Zimbabwe

OPEC
Algeria
Ecuador
Gabon
Indonesia
Iran
Iraq
Kuwait
Libya
Nigeria
Qatar
Saudi Arabia
UAE
Venezuela

GLOSSARY

CLIMATE AND WEATHER
Drought Long period during which there is insufficient rainfall to support life and agriculture.
Equatorial climate Found at the Equator – high temperatures and plentiful rain throughout the year.
Mediterranean climate Like that around the Mediterranean Sea – hot, dry summers and warm, wet winters.
Temperate climate Lacking extremes of temperature; neither hot nor cold.
Tropical climate Found close to the Equator – hot all year round with abundant rainfall.

ECONOMIC TERMS
Developed country One which is industrially and economically advanced.
Exports Goods sold outside the country in which they were produced.
Gross national product (GNP) The total value of all goods and services produced by a country (usually in a year).
Imports Goods from one country brought into another to be sold.
Industrialized nation One which has well-developed industry as an important part of its economy.
Inflation Sudden rise in prices caused by availability of too much money.
Manufactured goods Made from raw materials or individual components either by hand or by machines.
Per capita A head, each.
Resources Materials that meet a need, e.g. iron ore to make steel, or good soil for growing crops.
Underdeveloped nation One which has not yet developed a high level of industry to support its economy.

ETHNIC GROUPS
Caucasoid Belonging to the group of "white-skinned" people; usually called "whites".
Mongoloid Belonging to the group of people characterized by yellowish skin, slanting eyes and dark hair.
Negroid Belonging to the group of people with dark-skin and dark hair; usually called "blacks".
Pygmies Dwarf-like, dark-skinned people living in Africa or Asia (Negritos).
Veddoid From the Vedda (Veddah) people; ancient aboriginal race of Sri Lanka, now merged with modern Sinhalese people.

GEOGRAPHICAL TERMS
Desert Region with very little rainfall and few plants and animals; usually sandy. It may be either hot or cold.
Equator Imaginary line encircling the middle of the Earth.
Famine Severe lack of food usually caused by crop failure or drought.
Hydroelectricity Electricity produced by using water power.

Irrigation System of bringing water for agriculture from a place where it is plentiful to a place where it is scarce.
Peninsula Spur of land nearly surrounded by water.
Population density Average number of people living in a square kilometre (or mile), calculated by dividing the population of a country by its area.
Rural Based in the countryside rather than in the towns.
Savanna Land with grassy plains and few or no trees, often found between equatorial forests and hot deserts.
Tropical rainforest Forest in the tropics with trees that thrive on heavy rainfall; often called jungle.
Urban Based in towns rather than in the countryside.
Volcano Cone-shaped opening in the Earth's crust, through which molten rock (lava) comes to the surface.
Ved South African open country, uncultivated grasslands.

RELIGIONS
Christianity Based on teachings of Jesus Christ and his followers. Practised by Protestants and Roman Catholics.
Islam Based on the teachings of Mohammed, practised mainly among Arabs and Africans. Its followers are called Muslims.
Judaism Based on the teachings of Moses. Its followers are called Jews.

TYPES OF GOVERNMENT AND POLITICAL TERMS
Apartheid Segregation of black and white people, practised in South Africa.
Colony Place settled by people who go to live there, but who remain citizens of their country of birth.
Civil war War between groups of citizens of the same country.
Coup Sudden seizure of power from an elected government by a group such as the military.
Guerrillas Soldiers who are not part of a regular army but who harrass the enemy by surprise raids and sabotage.
Military Government Sometimes unelected, supported by the force of the military.
Monarchy Government by a monarcy (king or queen). In some, the power is limited, as in Britain or Sweden.
Republic Country in which the people elect the head of state and the government.

INDEX

All entries in bold are found in the Glossary

Photographic Credits:
(l=left, r=right, t=top, b=bottom, m=middle)
Contents page and pages 4 (both), 7 (all), 9 (t), 11 (l), 21, 22 (b), 25 (b), 29 (b) and 34: Robert Harding Library; pages 6 (both), 8 (l), 9 (l), 11 (t), 12 (both), 14 (t), 15 (t), 17 (all), 19 (all), 22 (r), 23 (both), 25 (t), 26 (both), 27 (b), 30 (t and b), 31 (both), 32 (both) and 33 (r): Hutchison Library; page 8 (r): NHPA; pages 11 (r), 13 (t), 14 (b), 15 (b), 26 (b), 29 (t) and 33 (l): Spectrum; pages 13 (b), 18 (b) and 27 (t): Frank Spooner Agency; pages 22 (l) and 30 (m): Rex Features.